Supersonic SOUNDS
PHONEME PRACTICE

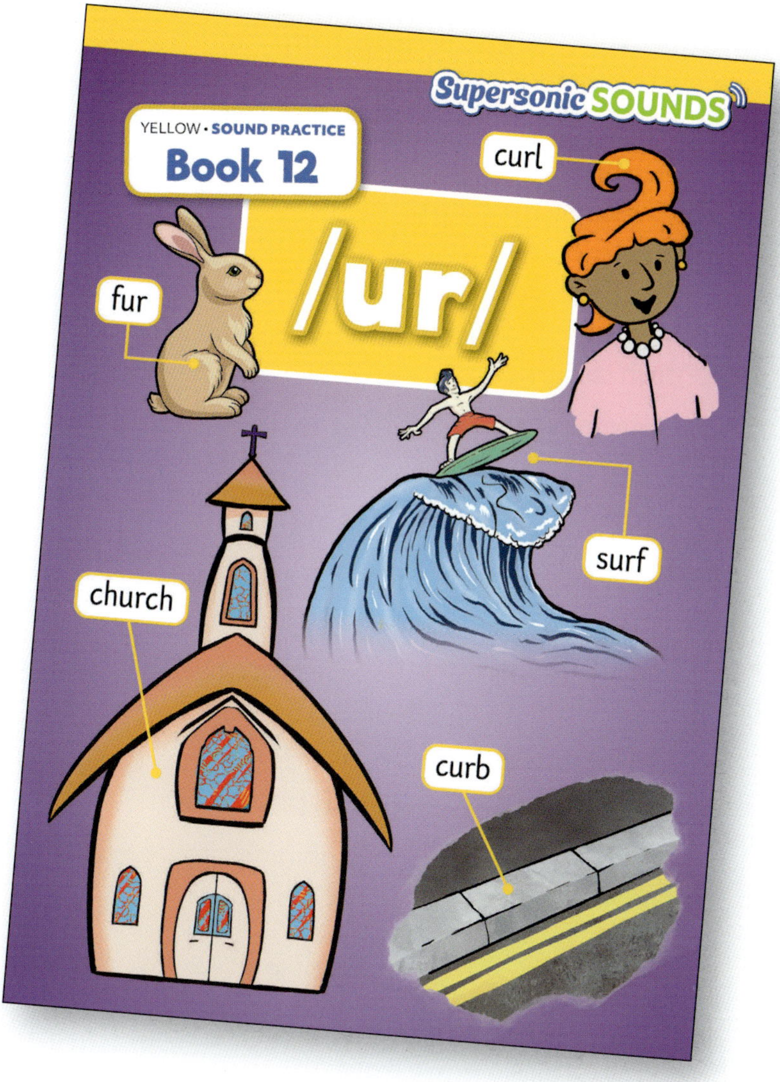

BEARPO
PUBLISH
T0389878
Minneapolis, Min

Teaching Tips

This book focuses on the phoneme **/ur/**.

Getting Started

- Review the focus phoneme of the book with readers.
- Model the sound and have readers practice themselves.

Using the Book

- Ask readers to read the words on the pages with the colorful borders, using the focus sound as their guide.
- Turn the page and check the illustration next to the word to confirm accuracy.
- As you read new words, review the word bank on the left-hand pages of the book.

Reviewing

- Encourage readers to independently reread all of the words on pages 22–23.
- Have them complete the activity on page 24 for continued practice with the focus phoneme.
- Extend the learning by asking readers if they know any other words containing the focus phoneme.

© 2025 Booklife Publishing
This edition is published by arrangement with Booklife Publishing.

North American adaptations © 2025 Bearport Publishing Company. All rights reserved. No part of this publication may be reproduced in whole or in part, stored in any retrieval system, or transmitted in any form or by any means, electronic, mechanical, photocopying, recording, or otherwise, without written permission from the publisher. Bearport Publishing is a division of Chrysalis Education Group.

For more information, write to Bearport Publishing, 5357 Penn Avenue South, Minneapolis, MN 55419.

curb

curb

curb

curl

curl

curl

curb

curl

fur

fur

fur

curb

curl

fur

surf

surf

surf

curb

curl

fur

surf

church

church

church

curb

curl

fur

surf

church

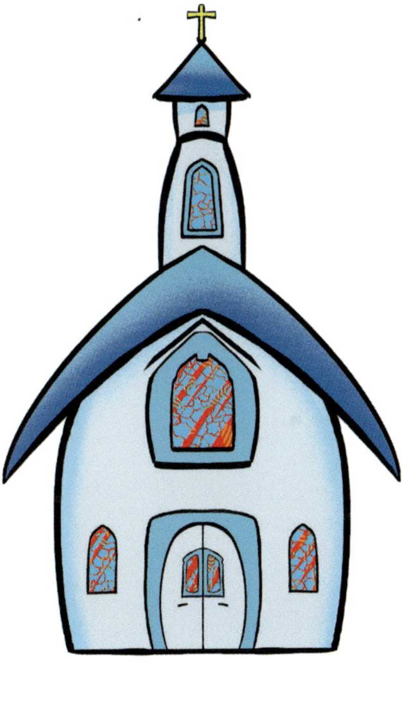

Say the sound and trace the letters with your finger.

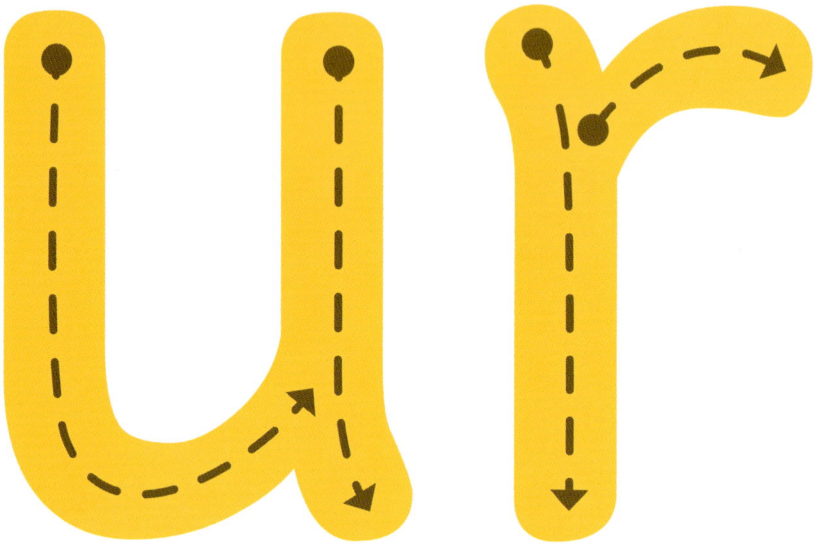